MEL BAY PRESENTS

IMPROVISING WITHO

MW00862384

The Intervallic Guitar System
of CARL VERHEYEN

CD contents

1	Major Example 1	21	Minor Example 1	41	Dominant Example 1
2	Major Example 2	22	Minor Example 2	42	Dominant Example 2
3	Major Example 3	23	Minor Example 3	43	Dominant Example 3
4	Major Example 4	24	Minor Example 4	44	Dominant Example 4
5	Major Example 5	25	Minor Example 5	45	Dominant Example 5
6	Major Example 6	26	Minor Example 6	46	Dominant Example 6
7	Major Example 7	27	Minor Example 7	47	Dominant Example 7
8	Major Example 8	28	Minor Example 8	48	Dominant Example 8
9	Major Example 9	29	Minor Example 9	49	Dominant Example 9
10	Major Example 10	30	Minor Example 10	50	Dominant Example 10
11	Major Example 11	31	Minor Example 11	51	Dominant Example 11
12	Major Example 12	32	Minor Example 12	52	Dominant Example 12
13	Major Example 13	33	Minor Example 13	53	Dominant Example 13
14	Major Example 14	34	Minor Example 14	54	Dominant Example 14
15	Major Example 15	35	Minor Example 15	55	Dominant Example 15
16	Major Example 16	36	Minor Example 16	56	Dominant Example 16
17	Major Example 17	37	Minor Example 17	57	Dominant Example 17
18	Major Example 18	38	Minor Example 18	58	Dominant Example 18
19	Major Example 19	39	Minor Example 19	59	Dominant Example 19
20	Major Example 20	40	Minor Example 20	60	Dominant Example 20

Contents

In the Beginning 3

The Integrity of the Line 4

The Proximity Factor 4

Make Music Sound Different 5

The Lines 5

The Intervals 6

Melodic Direction 9

Major Key Lines 10

Minor Key Lines 17

Dominant 7th Key Lines 24

Coda 32

In the Beginning

In the early part of 1980, I found myself at a musical crossroads. I had played in rock bands since I was 11 years old, worked as a solo or duo acoustic performer in bars since the legal age of 18 and done my share of pop and rock 'n roll club work. Then in my 20s I immersed myself in the world of jazz. I studied bebop and the fine art of playing over changes while leading an original band, playing two nights a week for four years. And I was currently taking classical guitar lessons from a friend, transcribing Chet Atkins solos, expanding my jazz repertoire and delving into the world of country and bluegrass. I had played 1000 gigs, keeping up my string bending and blues chops as well.

But something told me there was a new style; a modern approach to improvising that would transcend stylistic pigeonholes and have relevance within all types of music. Wayne Shorter inspired me, playing on the Joni Mitchell records and on the track "Aja" by Steely Dan. I was inspired by Joe Zawinul's playing in Weather Report, and seeing them live with Jaco Pastorius rocked as hard as Cream had done in the late 60s. I needed a new musical language that paid tribute to the various styles I had worked hard to incorporate into my playing, but one to which I could truly relate. I needed a language of my era, as bebop had been to the 40s. A modern approach to improvising not bound by the guitar or any one particular style of music. An all encompassing direction and musical philosophy that worked over the chord changes found in the jazz standards I knew as well as the single key vamps found in rock 'n roll.

As we often do in our musical development, I hit a plateau where things began to come together. I could reference many wonderful influences, and had no problem combining styles like that of Chet Atkins and Keith Richards to form useful hybrids, a vocabulary for studio work. In the studio, a little bit of Jimi Hendrix combined with some Andy Summers can make for a nice rhythm track. But as the working musician in me began to clash with my artistic sense, something unique began to take shape in the practice room. A style began to crystallize and for the first time I could recognize various elements that were my own.

Although I did not recognize it at the time, the defining moment on this path of self-discovery was a lesson some years earlier with the great jazz guitarist Joe Diorio. He introduced me to the idea of an ongoing musical diary or lick book, and the discipline of daily updates as a means of harmonic exploration. The simple concept is this: As you practice you write down the lines and musical ideas that sound like your own.

The Integrity of the Line

Then I asked myself these questions: Why do I like various improvising musicians like Albert King, Herbie Hancock, Pat Martino, Joe Zawinul and Eddie Van Halen? How do these guys make music sound different? The answer seemed to point to the lines, the musical sentences with which they speak. Above all other considerations like tone and musical genre; the integrity of the line is the key element. The integrity of the line is what separates the melodic players from the lick players. The integrity of the line is the difference between unintelligible garble and a fully developed story. In guitar speak: it is the difference between wanking and saying something!

So I threw out all my scales and arpeggios, vowing never to practice these static, unusable forms again. My concept then centered on the idea that there are NO EXERCISES. There is nothing we should be practicing that we can't use in improvisation. Why practice an exercise of a C major scale ascending in 6ths when we could play a melodic line using 6ths, 2nds and other intervals for use over a C major chord? In short, why study to become a musician when one can spend the time being a musician? During a typical practice session there is a lot of time wasted on non-creative busy work. The ultimate goal is this: Don't practice anything that can't be used on the stage. I am not saying that it isn't good to know how the major scale can ascend using the 6th interval, but there is no reason to practice music or exercises that you won't ultimately play.

In deconstructing the scales and putting them back together to create my own improvising vocabulary, I followed a few simple guidelines. The note we choose to follow the previous note is like the color a painter uses next to another color. It has a little to do with technique and a lot to do with expression. I listen and sing and play and listen, carefully running a line to hear if it could be improved by changing just one or two notes. I include the appropriate bends and slides, hammer-ons and pull-offs to give it character, staying true to my blues-rock-based ideal. Then I try to incorporate it into my existing lyrical statements, accessing a difficult starting phrase from a previous phrase that I already have under my hands. Expression and passion are the ultimate goals. Does the line make me feel something when I hear it? Does it go somewhere new while still being rooted in a recognizable form that draws the listener in?

Throughout the years I have filled many volumes of the lick books and they in themselves are the inspiration for this book. For me they are also a means to better and more concentrated practicing. If I wake up with absolutely nothing to work on or no inspiration at all I can always turn back a few pages to see what I was working on a few weeks ago. And since not everything I come up with will make it under my hands and into my playing, there are invariably quite a few things that get passed over. These ideas may become the seeds for future themes. Throughout the book you will see where I have taken a strong melodic "theme" and expanded it with many variations. Often times the variation is much better than the original idea, the extrapolation becomes the new theme to be built upon and expanded.

The Proximity Factor

I believe the guitar is an unlimited instrument, capable of so much more than we steadily hear out there. But for many players, a major limiting factor is the linear layout of the notes on the fretboard, the proximity of half steps and whole steps. For a keyboard player to play wider intervals, the physical effort is minimal. It takes one finger to make one note and the next note, say a major 7th above, can come from a completely different hand if necessary. But for the guitarist to play a single note, two hands must coordinate to strike at the same time and calculate the many minute distances horizontally between the frets (left hand) and vertically between the strings (right hand) before that next note, a major 7th above, can be played. It's no wonder we guitarists tend to play in a scalar fashion. It's a lot easier to stay on the same string! We learn our pentatonics and then our major, minor and dominant scales in a whole step-half step order as they are laid out in the various "boxes" and we tend to keep them that way. Then we learn the modes the same way, compounding the problem. But truly melodic playing is the deviation from that limitation. True melodic playing is the breaking out of those boxes.

I am constantly reminded of this when I hear guitarists playing the top three strings of the instrument in a single position. I want to hear a player take in the entire guitar from the deep low end to the screaming high end. I want to hear a guitarist play intervals greater than a minor 3rd. I want to hear a musical phrase that is longer than one or two bars. I am looking to hear a direction, a sense of style, and an attitude in the bends and vibrato. And I love to hear the story, unfolding naturally from beginning to end.

Make Music Sound Different

We must always keep reminding ourselves that as creative musicians, it is our job to make music sound different. As I listen to myself play in real time or on a recorded playback, I question each line as to its originality. Many times I will hear my various influences and that is okay. We emulate our favorite players for many years before our own styles emerge. But how are we shaping these influences and re-sculpting them to become a musical influence? How are we pushing the envelope? When I play the guitar I want people to know it is me within 4 or 5 notes. I do not always achieve this high level of creative originality, but it is a constant goal.

When I decided to title this book "Improvising Without Scales." I knew there would be a lot of questions. For this reason I have divided the book into three main chapters: Major, Minor and Dominant. Obviously I know my major, minor and dominant scales and well as the modes, diminished and altered scales. But the book's title evolved from the concept of deconstructing those linear forms to find a personal voice within them, and by no means endorses bypassing the harmonic knowledge gained from learning them.

The Lines

I encourage you to play the examples with the fingerings that I use because this is often a big part of the sound. All of them can be played clean or with distortion, with vibrato and bending, even on acoustic guitar. But I think all guitarists should have a good clean, undistorted amp at home to really listen to the sound their hands are making on the electric guitar. I believe it is good to practice both clean and with distortion to let your ears and hands react to the different amounts of sustain available. Our hands can create sustain, with practice. The goal is to achieve a singing quality with both types of sound.

Not all of these ideas can be transposed. Some have too much fret range or are just too long. But for the shorter lines, I highly recommend transposition. It will open up many more doors.

Consider every line you learn, whether it's one of the examples in this book or an original phrase, as "money in the bank." It is material you can draw on whenever you find yourself in an improvising situation with a given tonal center. I believe the very best of us are only truly improvising about 30% of the time. The rest of the time we are playing things we have worked out, phrases we know and have under our hands. A wonderful side effect of perusing one's own stylistic direction is this: eventually you begin to improvise in that style. It makes perfect sense, the more you work on your direction, the more you sound like you.

5

The Intervals

The first step is to know and understand the basic sound of the intervals. Each one has a very different musical quality. The perfectly timed execution of a descending major 6th in a line can be breathtaking. An ascending line that breaks into 5ths at the end can have a dramatic impact, too. It's important to hear these sounds in your head first.

I am skipping 2nds because you already play this interval while practicing your scales. Look at example 1.1 and play this line. Composed almost entirely of major and minor 3rds, it has a unique characteristic about it. As you can probably tell right away, 3rds are the interval most commonly associated with the arpeggio. Notice how different it sounds from a scale oriented line. And musically, it is immediately more memorable than a scalar line, as well.

Example 1.1 - Line in thirds.

Now listen to example 1.2, an F#m line constructed of perfect 4th. I hear an angular, abstract tonality with this interval. There are no minor or major qualities. Its rigid structure makes it very powerful. And musically it's immediately more memorable, too.

Example 1.2 - Line in fourths.

The next interval, commonly known as the flat 5 or tritone, has a radical sound when played alone. This line for E7#9 sounds "outside" even with the chordal accompaniment. But used sparingly it can make your solo turn an unexpected corner. Because the tritone embodies that strong element of tension found in the V chord, it also contains the power of resolution when played before resolving to the I chord.

Example 1.3 - Line in flat fifths.

Play example 1.4 and hear the hollow, open sound of the 5th. As the space between the notes gets bigger, the more distance we cover on the fingerboard. This may involve some position changing practice.

Example 1.4 - Line in fifths.

The next two examples use major and minor 6ths. Much like 3rds, 6ths have a very musical and sonorous sound, perfectly suited to western harmony. Here is a typical G major R&B lick you've heard a thousand times.

Example 1.5 - R&B Line in sixths.

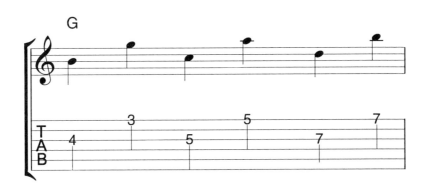

Now listen to a more non-traditional line using the 6th interval. The last two notes are a 4th finger slide from the 9th to the 17th fret.

Example 1.6 - Line in sixths

The next line uses a combination of major and minor 7th intervals in a descending dominant run. This discordant cascade finally resolves into the 3rd and then the root of the G7 chord, but along the way the line sounds "outside." Actually these clashing tones are completely diatonic, it's the intervals that make them sound strange.

Example 1.7 - Line in sevenths.

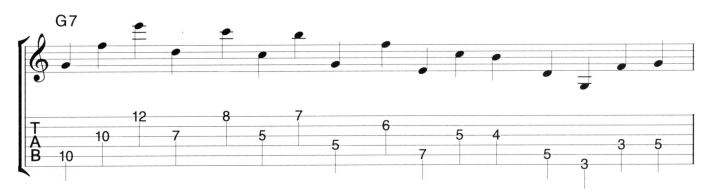

Listen to the next line using octaves. This is an interval I use sparingly due to its lack of color. Although I do find it useful for instant register jumps, it is the 10th between notes 4 and 5 that make this line musical to my ears.

Example 1.8 - Line in octaves.

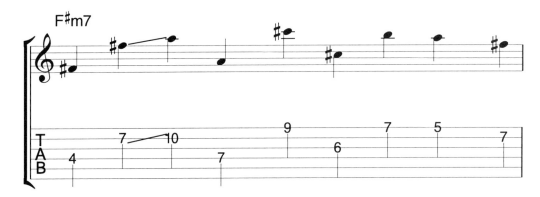

Although I do use the 9th and the 10th in my playing, it is these intervals (the 3rd through the octave) from which I get the most mileage. As you will see from the major, minor and dominant examples in the book, I never use a single interval repeatedly in my lines, preferring to mix them up in a more random, musical way. Use the knowledge of these sounds to make your own lines, make music sound different!

Melodic Direction

After the intervals themselves, the next most important criterion in line development is the melodic direction. Lines should ascend and descend, and technique should never limit our ability to do one or the other. Scale practice often molds the average guitarist into a directional soloist. It makes sense that if you practice your scales it is the scales themselves that become your lines, by virtue of the fact that they can be executed with the greatest speed and dexterity. We play the stuff we know, and the stuff we are good at.

Therefore I believe in constructing my lines with considerable care in the area of melodic direction. Look at example 1.9. The first three tones are ascending and then it drops down a minor 3rd. From the A to the F we are going up again followed by three notes in a row descending and three more ascending. The line goes up and down for awhile before ending in a blues lick.

I have talked to many famous soloists over the years about this. Some have told me they never go more than three notes in any one direction. But I believe that, too is a limitation and prefer to use my ear and taste to dictate the contour of the lines. No limits!

Example 1.9

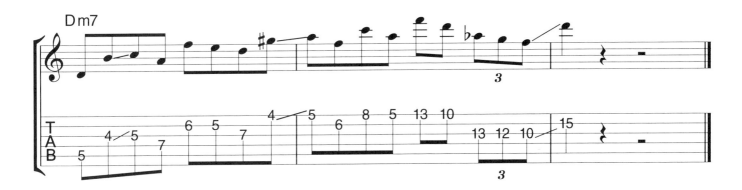

Major Key Lines

I like the open, pastoral sound of the major pentatonic scale with the 4th and the 9th added. By not using the major 7th we establish this unique quality that is not jazz or country.

The following examples are played at the beginning of each CD track.
The remainder of the track is an improvisation around that idea.

Major Example 1

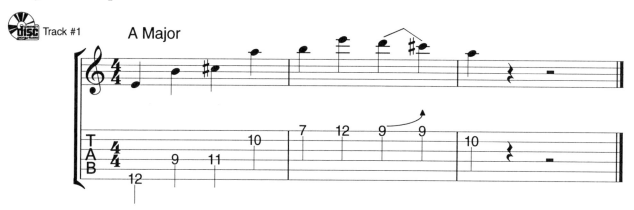

Major Example 2

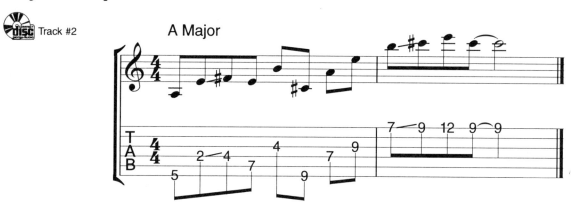

Sliding provides an expressive alternative to bends and hammer-ons. It also facilitates position changing, which enables the left hand to cover more of the fret board and couple ideas together. There are many ways to finger this line and each fingering sounds different, but try it this way first.

Major Example 3

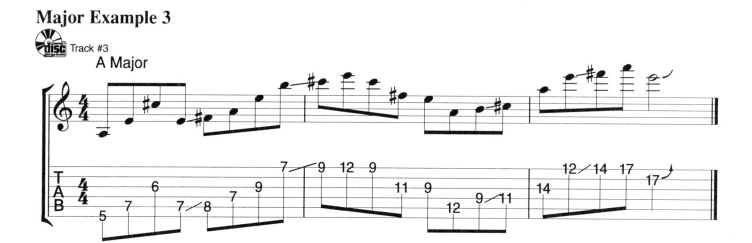

Although unintended in the linear arc of this line, the position changes seem to coincide with chord inversions. Hybrid picking (pick, middle and ring fingers) make the second bar a lot easier.

Major Example 4

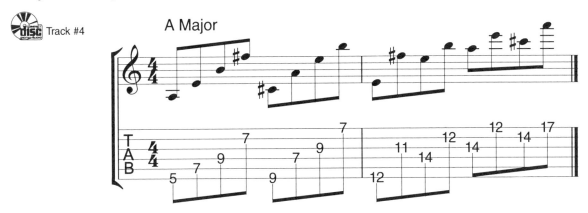

Using the last half of Major Example 4, we can compose a new line reversing the melodic direction.

Major Example 5

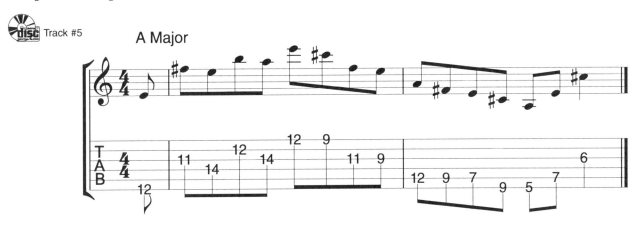

The interval between the 3rd and 4th notes in this next example is just short of two octaves, yet it sounds totally natural in this context.

Major Example 6

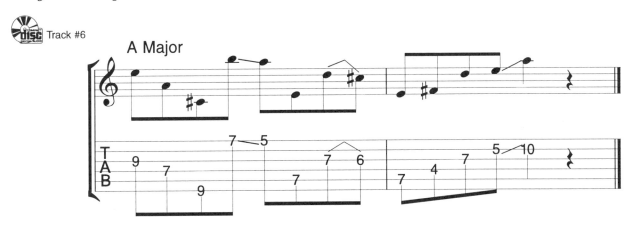

Borrowing the opening phrase from the previous example, I changed to a triplet rhythm to accent the cascading quality. Try it with straight 8th notes, too.

Major Example 7

Track #7

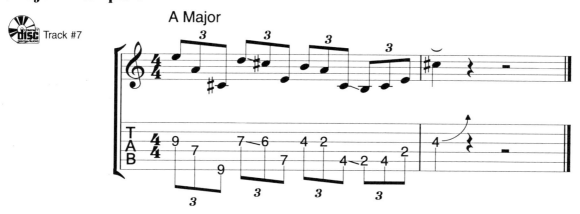

I have used this next line on two of my records. You can hear it in the solo on "Adult Chords" from the *No Borders* CD and in "Come Down Tonight" from *SIX*.

Major Example 8

Track #8

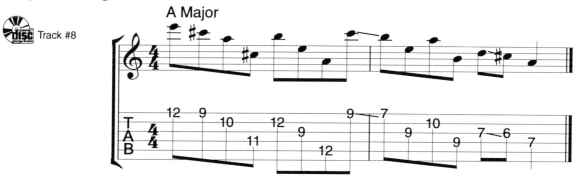

This is a musical ramp I use before Major Example 8. It also works before Major Example 9. On the CD you'll hear it coupled with Major Example 8.

Major Example 9   Track #9

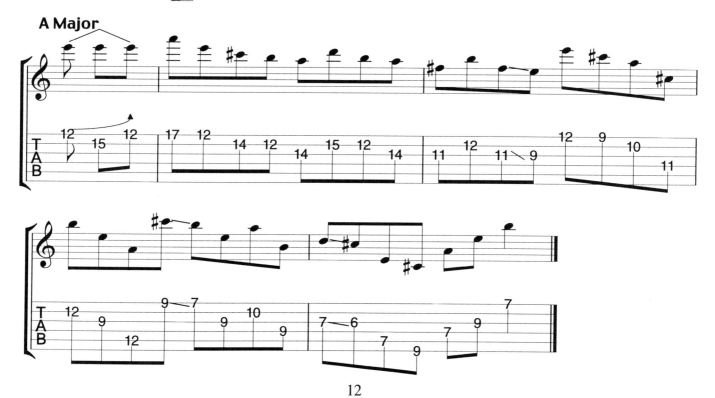

This line covers a lot of ground. Notice how it begins using Major Example 1 in triplets.

Major Example 10

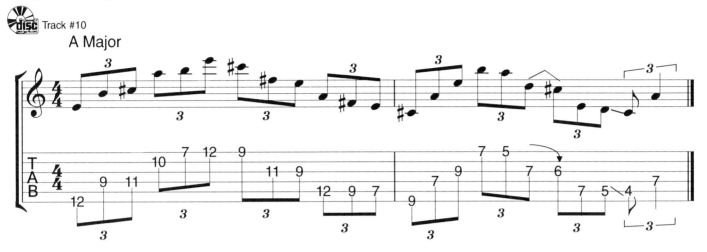

This line shows how a few well-placed intervals can make an ordinary pentatonic lick sound different. Try taking your old standbys and reworking them this way.

Major Example 11

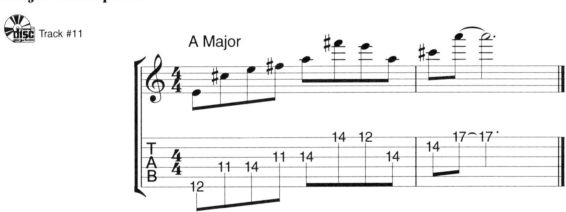

Sometimes the inspiration for a melodic idea can come from a chord form. I use the first 4 notes of this next line for an A2 chord. It seems to work without sounding like an arpeggio.

Major Example 12

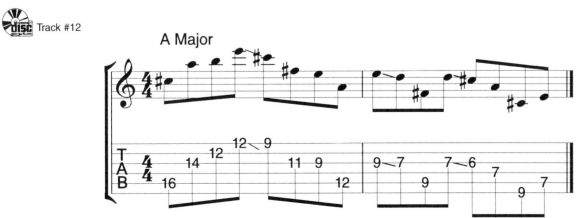

Using 6ths to start this line gives the descending pentatonic run a new twist. I like to end my lines using a position change.

Major Example 13

Here is another fingering for 6ths. This line can melodically set up some major pentatonic playing. It is a good place to begin a solo.

Major Example 14

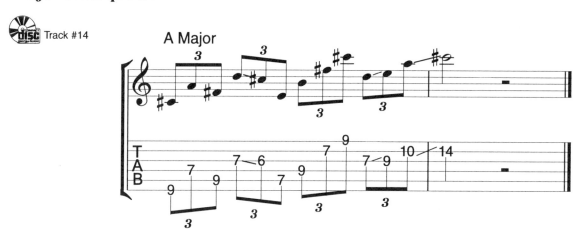

This is a rare example of line construction following a chord form (A7 sus). I do not use that technique too often because I do not want to sound like I am simply arpeggiating chords. You can also use this line for D major.

Major Example 15

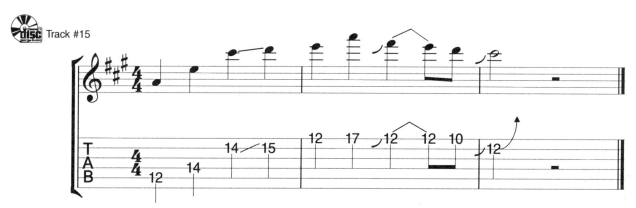

Here is a line I use for the opening melody in the song "Garage Sale", on the CD of the same name. Over the years I have seen many transcriptions with a lot of strange fingerings, but this is the correct way to play it, putting all the slides in the right place.

Major Example 16

Track #16 D Major

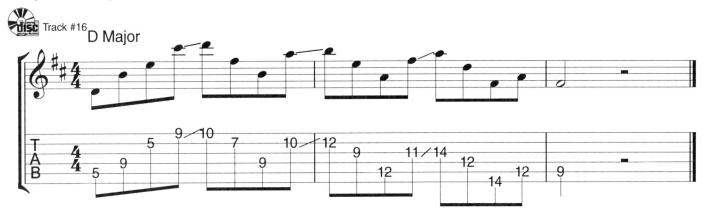

This ambiguous line works with many chords. I hear it over D major, but try it over the A major vamp, too.

Major Example 17

Track #17

D Major

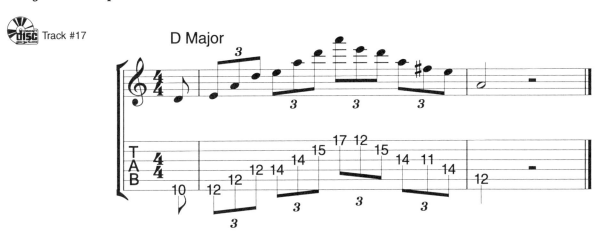

Changing just one note in an otherwise typical scalar run gives this line much more melodic range. In this case I took out a C♯ where the high G♯ now sounds (the 4th note of bar 2). Listen to the "before and after," when played fast you can really hear the difference.

Major Example 18

Track #18

E Major

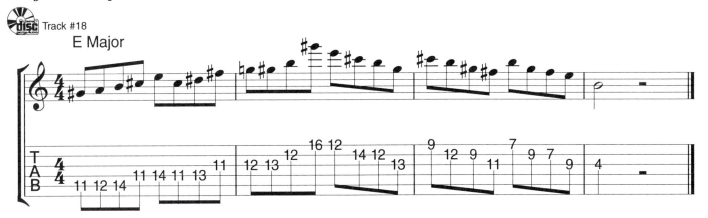

Another E major line with bends. Notice the C#m tonality in bar 2. With a few tweaks (like changing the low B to a C# in bar 2) this could have a minor application.

Major Example 19

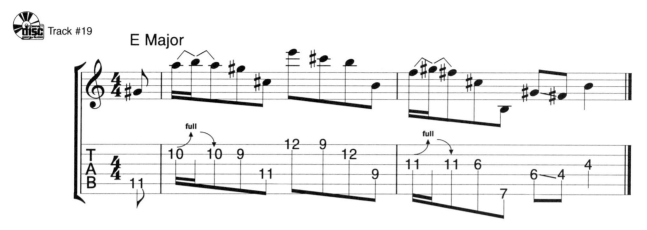

Track #19

E Major

Here is a good example of how much of the neck can be covered with the right position changes. The stair step sounding line in bars 2 and 3 uses 3rds, 4ths and 5ths.

Example Major 20

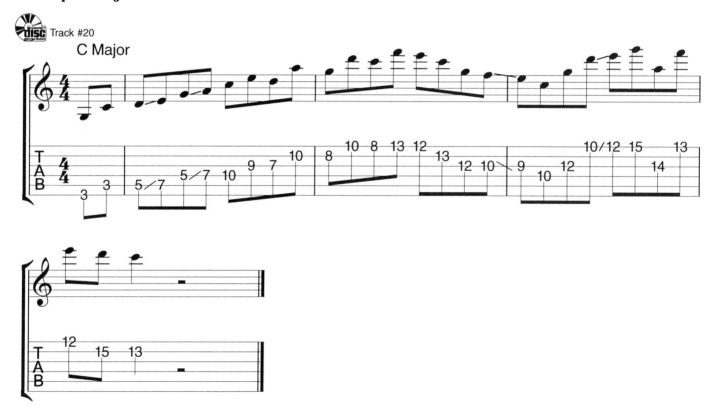

Track #20

C Major

16

Minor Key Lines

For the first minor line try something easy like skipping strings with a common pentatonic form.

Minor Example 1

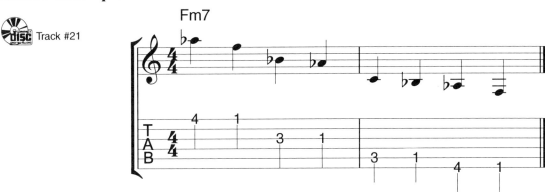

Next try it an octave up using the open B string to change from the 13th to the 1st position. To play it fast and seamlessly it helps to use a hybrid picking technique so you can get the open string with your 3rd finger on the right-hand.

Minor Example 2

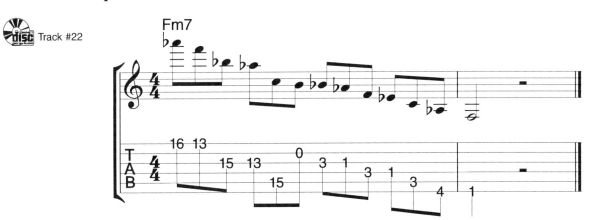

The following example is the bridge melody to my song "Lone Star" from the *Garage Sale* CD. Since the one, five, nine opening is neither major nor minor, I often use it to begin expansive lines ascending from the root.

Minor Example 3

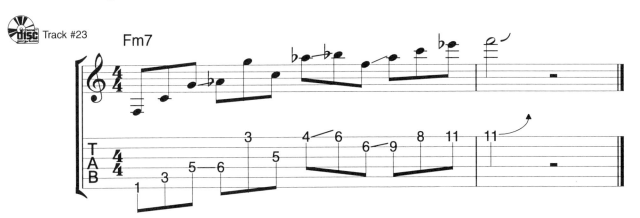

This line uses the one, five, nine opening beginning on the 3rd of the key. With a lot of stretching and a little practice you can make the radical position change and smooth it out nicely. The open 5ths have a very modern sound.

Minor Example 4

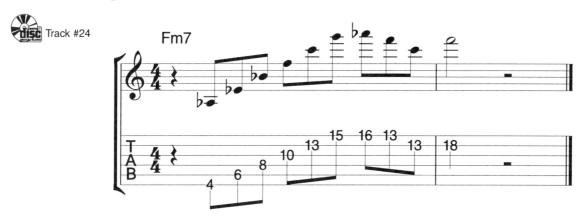

Starting on the 3rd again, this line repeats the stair step motif a few times before reaching the high F. Try it over an Am starting on a C.

Minor Example 5

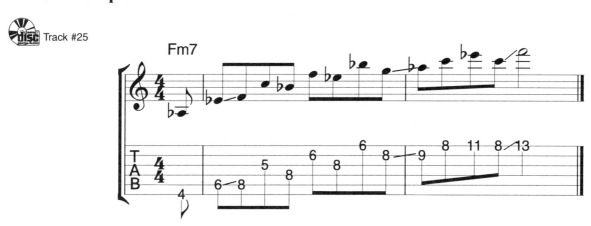

Here we can connect an Fm ascending run with the pentatonic position changing run from Minor Example 2, which sounds very different when played in a straight eighth rhythm.

Minor Example 6

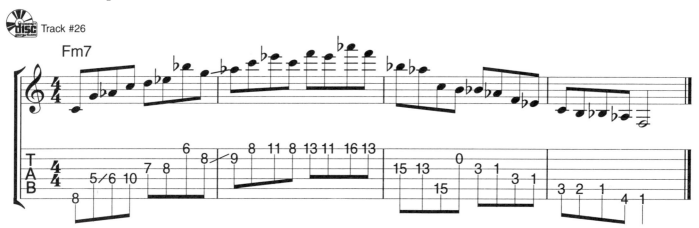

The low B in the second beat acts as an anchor note in this run.

Minor Example 7

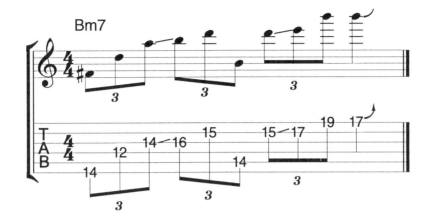

Beginning with an old standard pentatonic blues lick, this line immediately turns left by sliding down a whole step from F♯ to E in the 2nd triplet. The low B in bar two, beat 2 is played with the thumb if you can, and the last few notes are fingered exactly like the previous example.

Example Minor 8

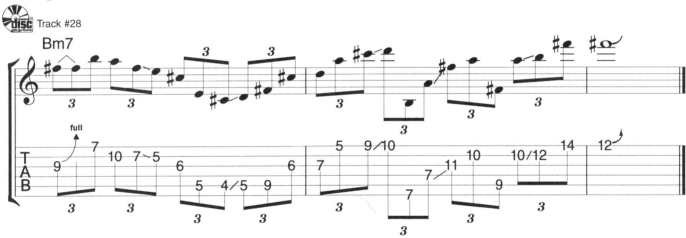

In this blues oriented line, the flat 5 of the key is the highest note. Once you have it down, transpose it up to Gm and end on a high G.

Minor Example 9

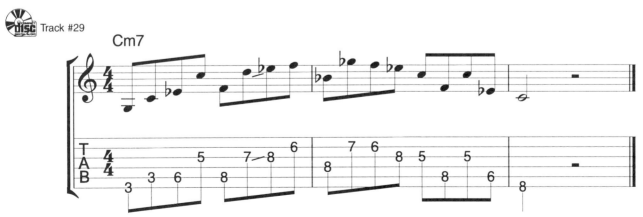

Ending with part of the previous line we can start with a blues lick and take it someplace new. I am constantly finding new directions by reworking past discoveries.

Minor Example 10

Track #30

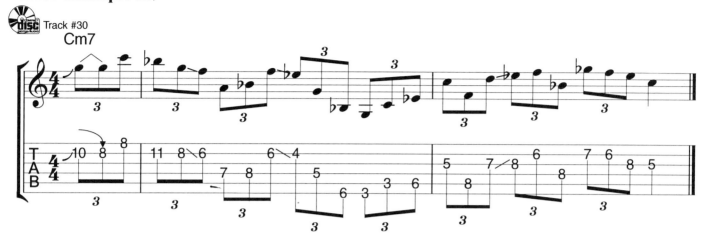

Here is a longer line that takes in the entire neck of the guitar. By alternately sliding with all four fingers (the 1st in bar one, the 4th in bar two, the 3rd and 2nd in bar three and the 4th and 3rd in bar four) this extensive range can be achieved. I use my thumb for the low C in the second bar.

Minor Example 11

Track #31

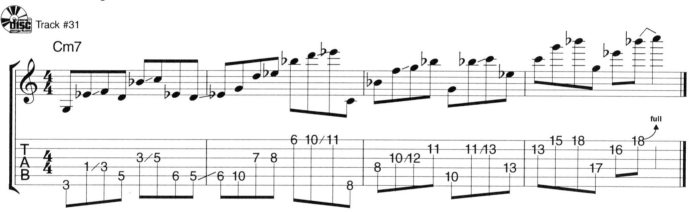

This is a simple line that uses a 6th and a 5th to start. I often use the first four notes in this line for my C2 or Am11 chord voicings. But I like the intervals so I turned it into useful melodic material.

Minor Example 12

Track #32

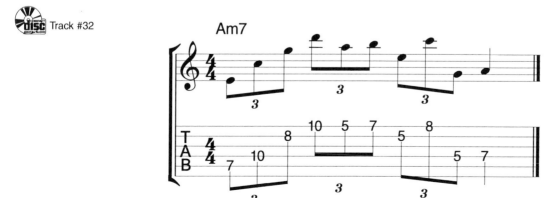

Some lines establish a vibe just by the juxtaposition of their intervals against the choice of notes. Using the flat 5 tone (bar one, beat 3) and the Major 7th interval (end of bar one) gives this line a dark, moody tone for Am.

Minor Example 13

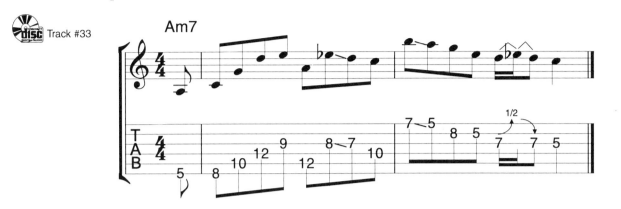

This line works in context of strong Dorian mode progressions. Bars three and four use a standard C Lydian arpeggio that also works for this relative minor application. Using hammer-ons and slides, find a way to make it as flowing and legato as possible. Finish with a solid bend up to the high A.

Minor Example 14

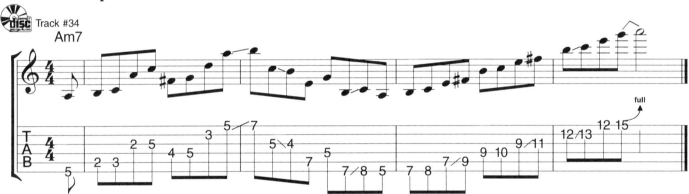

This line combines a high reaching Dm9 arpeggio with a ripping pentatonic lick. Try to continue the minor pentatonic line all the way down the neck using patterns on the 3rd and 4th strings.

Minor Example 15

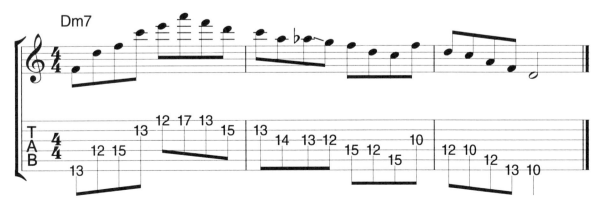

Here is another way out of the Dm9 line using slides.

Minor Example 16

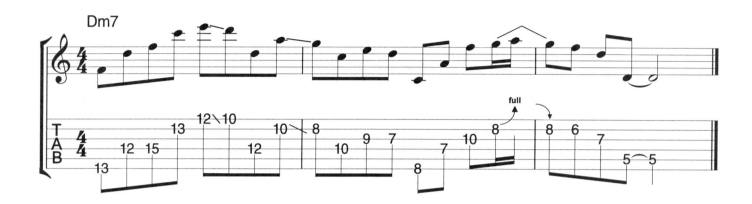

This line begins with some of the material I use all the time for minor and dominant chords. It blends nicely into some half step bends and then ends with the concept previously described in Minor Example 7.

Minor Example 17

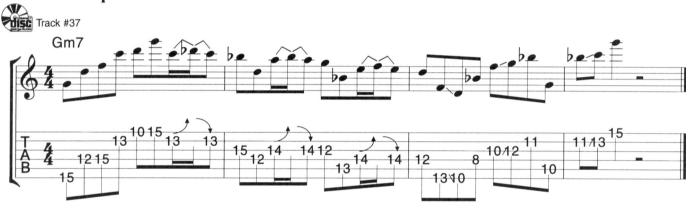

The next two lines climb through the tonal center of Em in very different ways. Minor Example 18 uses a low string slide into beat 3 of bar one. It helps if you can use your thumb for the "and of 4" in bar two. I finish with a pinch harmonic, making the final high E sound an octave higher.

Minor Example 18

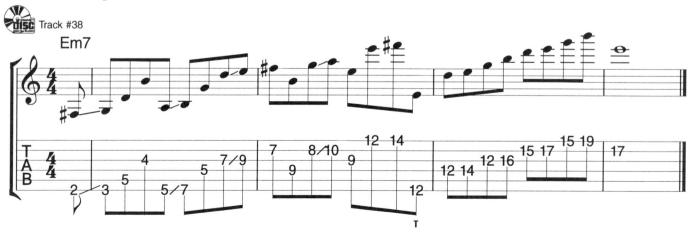

This slightly more complex line is interesting for the twists and turns it takes, constantly surprising the listener along the way. I take advantage of the thumb twice in this fingering. For an extra challenge try transposing the entire line up to Gm.

Minor Example 19  Track #39

Using slides we can climb from the 3rd to the 14th position in a melodic way. But the trip down is much faster using the open B string in the first beat of bar three. Over the years I have worked out open string inserts for every key. They give you the break you need to get your left hand from one end of the guitar to the other, facilitating a huge position change and a melodic line that does not sound like it could have possibly come from the guitar.

Minor Example 20  Track #40

Dominant 7th Key Lines

I believe a good dominant 7th line should have a certain amount of inherent tension so that the resolution is a pronounced melodic release. This first line has that tension, but it is also very melodic. I used something like this to start my solo on the track "Maggie's Ladder" from the *SIX* CD.

Dominant Example 1

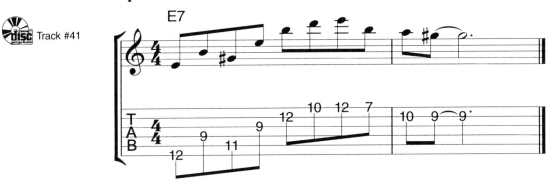

This simple line stays in one position, but the right hand picking takes some practice.

Dominant Example 2

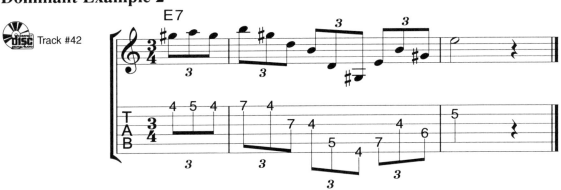

I use this sliding technique quite a bit to get up the neck. Watch for the position change at the end of the 3rd bar. It actually jumps to another idea here that I will explore in Dominant Example 8.

Dominant Example 3   Track #43

Here is a good example of reworking existing lines for alternate uses. The opening 6 notes are a major (or dominant) version of example 9 in the minor key chapter. I just changed the minor 3rd to a major 3rd and went in a new direction from there. The last 2 beats in bar one and the first 2 beats in bar two should all ring together.

Dominant Example 4 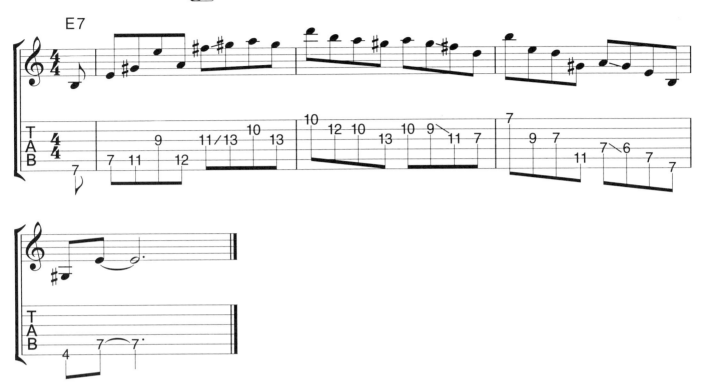 Track #44

This next line is a quirky set of four different abstract arpeggios. Try swinging it rhythmically.

Dominant Example 5 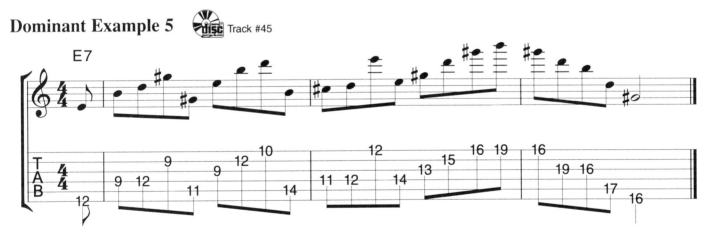 Track #45

By ending with a blues lick you can draw the listener in with familiar thematic material.

Dominant Example 6 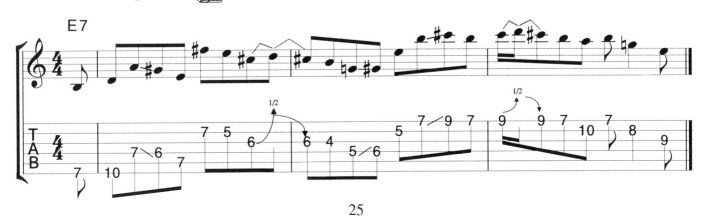 Track #46

This next line uses some typical scale oriented playing with the wide intervals of Dominant Example 2. Practice the jump from the end of bar 2 to the beginning of bar 3. It is a little rough at high speeds.

Dominant Example 7

Track #47

Here is an arpeggio style run I use extensively. You can here it on my solo for the track "Revival Downs" on the *Atlas Overload* CD.

Dominant Example 8

Track #48

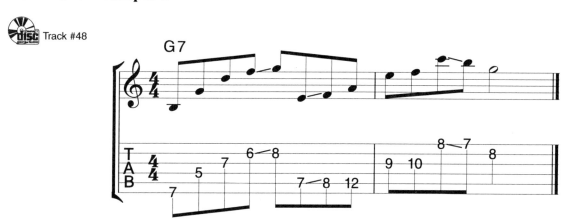

Accentuating the 7th while taking in almost 3 octaves. You can also end on a B, 7th fret 6th string.

Dominant Example 9

 Track #49

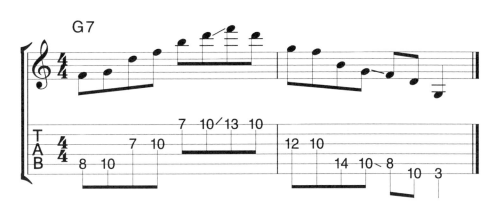

You may remember this stair step lick from example 4 in the Major Key chapter. Most of the major key material can be easily reworked for 7th chords.

Dominant Example 10

 Track #50

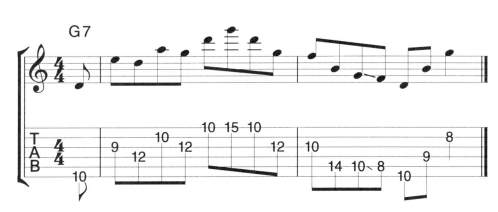

This simple phrase is the jumping off point for many great lines. Make sure you finger it this way. Try leaving out the last note (G) and skipping up to a Bb on the first string. From there you can descend with a minor Pentatonic run for a blues sound.

Dominant Example 11

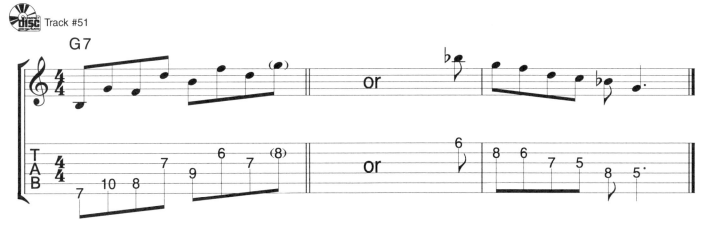 Track #51

I use the flat 3rd approach note into the major 3rd at the beginning of bars one and two. To end, I used another minor pentatonic ending but you can go many other places with this line. Practice it in all 12 keys.

Dominant Example 12

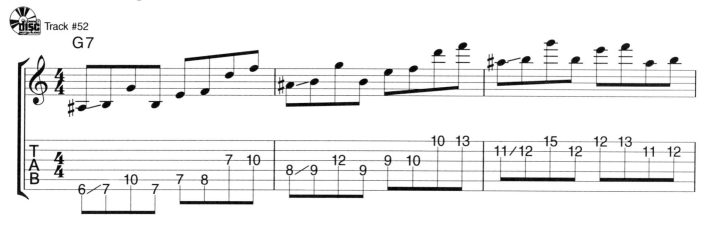

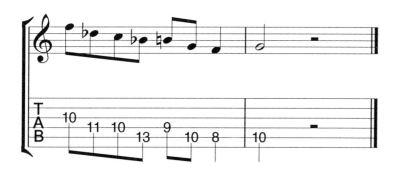

Here is another form that works for minor and dominant material. I combine it with an ending similar to the one used in example 10. Try barring with your first finger for the 1st and 2nd notes of the phrase, if your left thumb is not used to stretching over the top of the neck, or if you are physically unable to make this move.

Dominant Example 13

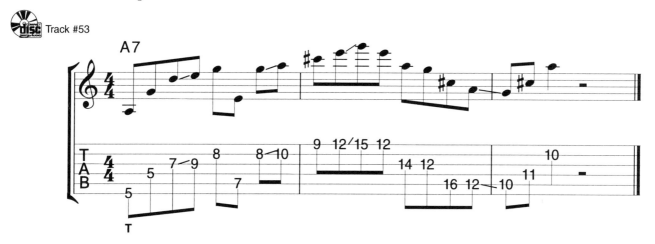

I used a similar line to this one on the last chorus of "No Walkin' Blues" from the *Slingshot* CD. I try to retain the blues feel while playing something different than the standard blues repertoire.

Dominant Example 14

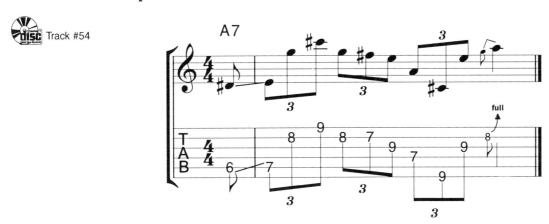

Track #54

This line seems to resolve within itself from the sus4 to the major 3rd. Notice the Am triad outlined in bar two.

Dominant Example 15

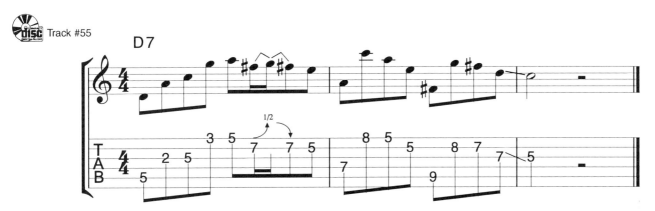

Track #55

Using the Am pentatonic as a basis for this line yields a rich dominant color, especially when we include the major 3rd on the descent. Although it's slightly scalar sounding, notice the hidden intervals: Major 3rd, 4th and 5th, minor and major 6th.

Dominant Example 16

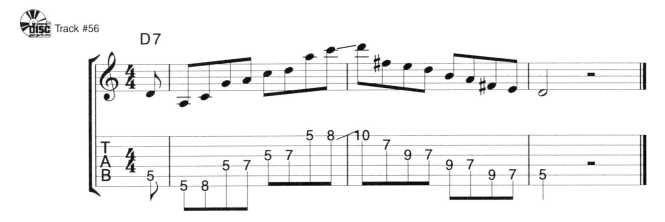

Track #56

The half step bends make this lick come alive. Listen to the CD for an idea of the phrasing.

Dominant Example 17

 Track #57

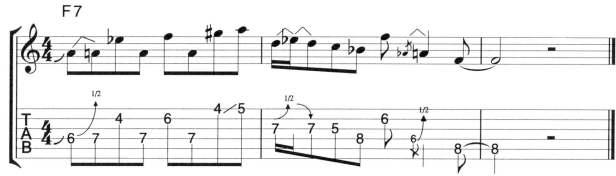

Another simple dominant blues lick, this one covers two octaves with a small amount of notes. Often times editing your playing can provide a more melodic end result. The notes you leave out are as important as the ones you play.

Dominant Example 18

 Track #58

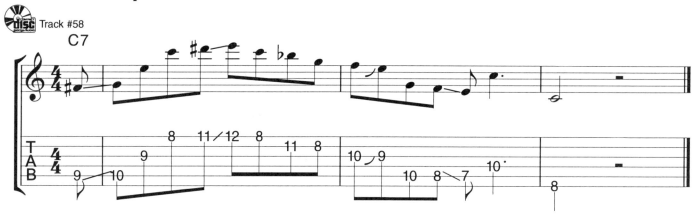

Borrow the funky opening from Dominant Example 14 and take it somewhere else. Here we end with some blues bends. This one sounds good with a swing funk feel.

Dominant Example 19

 Track #59

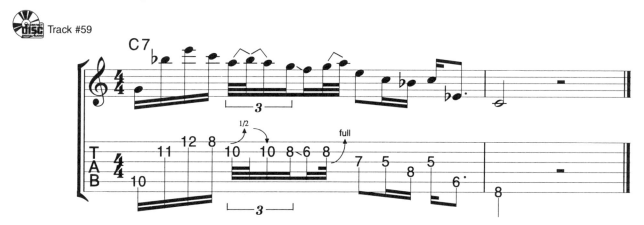

The arc of this line has a slightly discernible pattern to it, but not a rigid grid-like set of intervals. I prefer a more organic sound to something that sounds like math. When music reaches for perfection, its beauty is found in the striving.

Dominant Example 20

Track #60

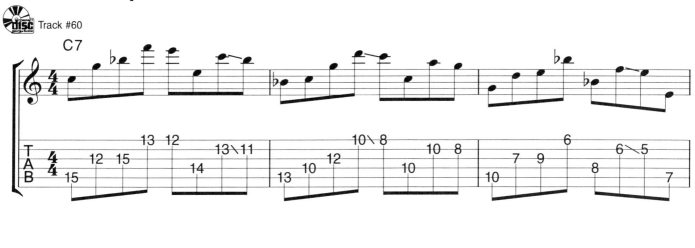

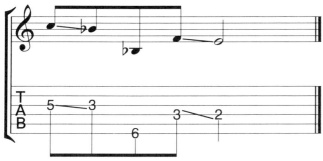

Coda

Start your own lick book. Begin by changing some of the notes in lines you have learned in this book to suit your taste. And then write them down. Challenge yourself to write new lines with goals like this:

1) I need a line for Am that starts on the high A on the 1st string and ends on the low C on the 6th string.

2) I need a B7 line that begins with a pentatonic blues lick and ends on the high B on the 19th fret.

These simple goals can be the beginnings of many creative avenues of harmonic discovery.

For me, the ultimate goal when improvising is to find yourself totally in the moment. You let go of all your inhibitions and play off the top of your head. This only happens when everything is right: the tone of your instrument, the balance of your sound within the ensemble, the amount of sleep you have had and many other subtle factors. To achieve this lofty space on stage I attempt to play the lines I know until I begin to hear the unknown lines. On a good night I can draw upon the material I have in a given tonal center and let it lead me to new places. This is truly a state of higher consciousness, much like meditation. I have often found myself back in the hotel room late in the evening after a show, trying to remember the new places I found tonight. And writing them down so that I can practice them tomorrow…

Good luck with your music,

Carl Verheyen

Visit Carl at www.CarlVerheyen.com